Things to Know About Loan Structuring

First published by Kjøller 2023

Table of Contents

Introduction

Loan structuring can sometimes feel like a complex process, with a myriad of confusing terms and jargon. It's not uncommon for people to feel overwhelmed or intimidated when faced with the task of taking out a loan or negotiating a new loan agreement. However, with the right knowledge and understanding of loan structuring, you can confidently navigate the process and make informed decisions that will benefit you in the long run.

This glossary-style book aims to provide readers with a clear and concise explanation of the key terms and concepts related to loan structuring. From the basics like interest rates and repayment terms, to more advanced topics such as collateral and covenants, each definition is presented in a straightforward manner that's easy to understand. Whether you're a borrower, lender, or simply interested in financial matters, this book will prove to be an invaluable resource that demystifies the world of loan structuring.

Accrual

Refers to the accumulation of interest over time on a loan. The interest that accrues on a loan is added to the principal balance, increasing the amount that the borrower owes.

Adjustable-Rate Mortgage (ARM)

A mortgage with an interest rate that changes periodically based on market conditions. ARM loans offer lower initial interest rates than fixed-rate loans, but the interest rate can fluctuate, leading to payment variability.

Advance Rate

The percentage of a loan that a lender is willing to provide. For example, if the advance rate is 80%, then a business can borrow up to 80% of the asset's value.

Amortization

A loan structuring technique where the borrower pays off the principal and interest in equal installments over a certain period of time. During the earlier years of the loan period, interest payments are higher and then decrease over time as the principal balance decreases.

Amortization Schedule

A table that shows the payment amount, interest, and principal for each payment period during the life of the loan. The table allows borrowers to see how their payments are allocated between interest and principal.

Amortizing Asset

An asset that is expected to depreciate or wear out over time. Using an amortizing loan structure to finance the purchase of the asset can ensure that the cash inflows generated by the asset are sufficient to repay the loan.

Amortizing Loan

A loan that is structured with a fixed payment schedule that pays down the principal and interest over the life of the loan. Different from balloon loans, which require a large payment at the end.

Annual Percentage Rate (APR)

A measure of the cost of credit expressed as a percentage rate. The APR includes the interest rate, fees, and any other charges associated with the loan. It provides borrowers with a standardized way of comparing loan offers.

Appraisal

An assessment of the value of an asset, such as real estate or equipment, which is used to determine the loan amount. Lenders typically use appraisals to ensure that the loan amount does not exceed the value of the asset.

Asset-Based Lending

A type of loan structuring that evaluates the borrower's assets, such as inventory, to determine the loan amount instead of solely relying on creditworthiness. Asset-based lending allows businesses to obtain financing based on their collateral, which can be useful for startups or companies with a weak credit history.

Balloon Payment

A large payment due at the end of a loan term, typically used for loans with longer repayment periods, such as mortgages or large business loans. The balloon payment is often much larger than the monthly payments made over the life of the loan and can create challenges for borrowers to meet the payment. Loan structuring involves understanding the risks involved with balloon payments and determining appropriate repayment plans.

Bankruptcy

A legal process that provides relief to individuals or businesses that cannot repay their debts. Bankruptcy can affect the loan structuring process as it impacts the borrower's creditworthiness and may require restructuring or renegotiation of loans.

Beneficiary

The party who receives the funds from a loan, typically the borrower. Loan structuring involves evaluating the borrower's financial situation to determine the appropriate loan amount and terms for the beneficiary.

Bond

A financial instrument used to raise capital through the issuance of securities. Bonds come with fixed interest rates and repayment dates and are often used by businesses and governments to finance large projects. Loan structuring involves understanding the risks and benefits of bond issuances and determining appropriate terms for borrowers.

Borrower

A party that receives a loan from a lender, typically to finance a project or purchase. The borrower is responsible for paying back the principal, interest, and other associated fees in a manner that is agreed upon in the loan agreement. Loan structuring involves understanding the borrower's financial situation, credit history, and repayment capabilities to determine appropriate loan terms.

Bridge Loan

A short-term loan used to finance a project or purchase immediately while waiting for long-term financing to become available. Bridge loans often come with higher interest rates and fees due to the increased risk involved. Loan structuring involves assessing the need for a bridge loan and determining appropriate loan terms.

Bullet Loan

A loan that requires the borrower to repay the entire principal amount in a single lump sum at the end of the loan term. This type of loan is often used for short-term financing needs and is not appropriate for longer-term projects. Loan structuring involves evaluating the need for a bullet loan and determining an appropriate repayment plan.

Business Plan

A document that outlines a company's goals, strategies, and financial projections. When applying for a loan, lenders often require a detailed business plan to evaluate the borrower's ability to repay the loan. Loan structuring involves reviewing the business plan to determine appropriate loan terms.

Business Valuation

The process of determining the value of a business for the purpose of buying or selling it, securing financing, or other business transactions. Loan structuring involves understanding the value of the borrower's business to determine the appropriate loan amount and terms.

Buyout

The process of acquiring a controlling interest in a company or business to take ownership of it. Buyouts are often funded through loans and are a common part of the loan structuring process. Loan structuring involves evaluating the risks and benefits of buyouts and determining appropriate loan terms.

Capital structure

A mix of debt and equity financing used by a borrower to fund its operations. The capital structure is an important consideration in loan structuring as it affects the borrower's creditworthiness and risk profile. A high level of debt in the capital structure can increase the risk of default and lower the credit rating, while a low level of debt can limit the borrowing capacity and growth potential.

Certification

A process of verifying the accuracy and completeness of financial statements and other documents provided by a borrower to a lender. Certification is an important step in loan structuring as it helps lenders to assess the risk of lending to a borrower and determine the loan amount and interest rate.

Collateral

A type of security that is pledged by a borrower to the lender as a guarantee of repayment of the loan. In loan structuring, collateral can include real estate, stocks, equipment, or any other valuable asset that can be liquidated in the event of default by the borrower. The value of the collateral is assessed by the lender to determine the loan amount and the interest rate.

Conditions

Terms and requirements specified by a lender as part of the loan agreement. Conditions can include collateral, covenants, interest rate, repayment schedule, and loan purpose. Conditions are negotiated by the borrower and the lender in loan structuring and are subject to change based on the performance of the borrower and the economic environment.

Cost of capital

The minimum rate of return required by a lender to compensate for the risk of lending money. The cost of capital is an important consideration in loan structuring as it affects the interest rate and the overall cost of borrowing. The cost of capital depends on various factors, such as the credit rating of the borrower, the collateral value, and the economic environment. Lenders use various tools and techniques to calculate the cost of capital, such as discounted cash flow analysis, comparative analysis, and historical data analysis.

Counterparty risk

The risk of loss to a lender due to the failure of another party, such as a guarantor, to fulfill its obligations under the loan agreement. Counterparty risk is an important consideration in loan structuring as it can affect the collateral requirements, covenants, and interest rate. Lenders use various tools and techniques to assess and manage counterparty risk, such as credit analysis, legal documentation, and collateral monitoring.

Covenants

A set of rules and restrictions that a borrower has to follow as part of the loan agreement. Covenants can include financial ratios, limitations on capital expenditures, and restrictions on dividend payments. Covenants help lenders to monitor the financial health of the borrower and minimize the risk of default.

Credit analysis

A process of evaluating the creditworthiness of a borrower by analyzing various financial and non-financial factors, such as income, assets, liabilities, credit history, and business plan. Credit analysis is an important step in loan structuring as it helps lenders to assess the risk of lending to a borrower and determine the loan amount and interest rate.

Credit rating

A numerical score assigned by credit rating agencies to borrowers based on their creditworthiness. The credit rating is an important factor considered by lenders in loan structuring as it determines the interest rate, collateral requirements, and covenants. A higher credit rating indicates a lower risk of default, and therefore, a better borrowing profile.

Credit risk

The risk of loss to a lender due to a borrower's failure to repay the loan. Credit risk is a key consideration in loan structuring as it determines the interest rate, collateral requirements, and covenants. Lenders use various tools and techniques to assess and manage credit risk, such as credit analysis, credit ratings, and loan loss provisions.

Debt Consolidation

Refers to the process of taking out a single loan to pay off multiple existing debts. Debt consolidation allows borrowers to lower their monthly payments, reduce their interest rates, and simplify their financial payments.

Debt Forgiveness

A process where a lender cancels some or all of the outstanding loan balance of the borrower. Debt forgiveness is usually granted in situations of extreme financial hardship or when the borrower is unable to repay their loan.

Debt Restructuring

The process of changing the existing terms and conditions of a loan to make it easier for the borrower to repay the loan. Debt restructuring can include options such as an extension of the loan term, a reduction in the interest rate, or a reduction in the loan principal.

Debt Service Coverage Ratio (DSCR)

A financial ratio used to determine the ability of a borrower to make their loan payments on time. DSCR is calculated by dividing the net operating income of the borrower by the total loan payments (principal plus interest) due in a given period.

Debt Yield

A metric that measures the risk associated with a commercial real estate loan. Debt yield is calculated as the net operating income of the property divided by the loan amount. A high debt yield indicates a lower risk for the lender.

Debt-to-Income Ratio (DTI)

A ratio used by lenders to determine whether a borrower is eligible for a loan. DTI is calculated by dividing the borrower's debt obligations by their gross monthly income.

Default

Refers to the failure of a borrower to meet the loan obligations as per the agreed terms and conditions. A default can result in the lender initiating legal actions against the borrower to recover the outstanding loan amount.

Down Payment

The amount of money paid upfront by the borrower when taking out a loan. A down payment reduces the total amount of the loan and is typically expressed as a percentage of the total loan amount.

Drawdown

Refers to the process of borrowing funds from a loan facility in stages or increments over a period of time. Drawdowns are usually subject to certain terms and conditions as agreed between the borrower and the lender.

Due Diligence

The process of conducting a detailed analysis of the borrower's financial capacity and creditworthiness to determine the risk associated with lending to the borrower. Due diligence is typically conducted by the lender before approving a loan.

Effective Interest Rate

The effective interest rate is the interest rate that is charged on a loan after taking into account any fees or other costs associated with the loan. This can be a useful metric to compare different loan options and to determine which loan is most cost-effective in the long run.

Endorsement

An endorsement is a guarantee of a loan that is provided by a third party. This can be used to provide additional security for the lender and can make it more likely that the loan will be approved. However, it can also increase the risk for the third party, who will be responsible for repaying the loan if the borrower is unable to do so.

Equity Financing

Equity financing relates to a type of loan structuring where investors provide capital in exchange for a stake in the project or company. This is often used for high-risk ventures that do not have the ability to immediately repay the loan. It can also provide additional expertise and knowledge to the project, making it more successful in the long run.

Equity Participation

Equity participation refers to a situation where investors provide capital in exchange for a share in the profits of a project or company. This can be used as an alternative to traditional debt financing and can provide more flexibility for the borrower. However, it can also be risky since the investors will be entitled to a share of the profits, even if the project is not successful.

Equity Value

Equity value is the value of a company's assets minus its liabilities. This can be used to determine the value of a project or company and can be important for determining the terms and conditions of a loan or investment.

Escrow Account

An escrow account is a special account that is used to hold funds that are used to cover the loan payments. This can be used to ensure that the borrower is able to make the payments, even if they experience fluctuations in their cash flow. It can also provide some protection for the lender, ensuring that the loan is repaid in a timely manner.

Exit Strategy

An exit strategy refers to the plan that is put in place to repay the loan. This is a critical part of loan structuring since it will determine the terms and conditions of the loan, as well as the amount of interest that will be charged. The exit strategy can be tied to a specific event, such as the sale of the project or company, or it can be based on a timeline, such as a fixed period for repayment.

Expected Return

The expected return is the amount of return that is expected from a loan or investment. This can be used to determine whether a loan or investment is worth pursuing and can help borrowers and investors make informed decisions about their options.

Facility fee

A fee charged by lenders to cover the costs of underwriting and administering a loan. Facility fees may be expressed as a percentage of the loan amount, or a flat fee, and may be payable upfront or over the term of the loan.

Fee coverage ratio

A financial ratio used to assess a company's ability to cover its ongoing operating expenses after certain one-time or non-recurring fees and expenses have been paid. Lenders may use this ratio in analyzing the risk of a loan and setting appropriate loan terms.

Financial covenants

Provisions in loan agreements that require the borrower to meet certain financial performance metrics, such as maintaining a certain level of working capital or limiting certain types of expenses. Financial covenants are designed to protect the lender's interests by ensuring the borrower has the ability to repay the loan.

Financial statement

A written record of a company's financial performance, including its income statement, balance sheet, and cash flow statement. Financial statements are a critical component of loan structuring as they provide lenders with insight into a company's financial health and ability to repay the loan.

Financing structure

The manner in which a loan is structured, including the size, term, and interest rate, as well as any covenants or collateral requirements. The financing structure can impact a borrower's ability to manage its cash flow and meet its financial obligations.

Fixed charge coverage ratio

A financial ratio used to assess a company's ability to meet its fixed financial obligations, such as loan payments or lease payments. The ratio is calculated by dividing a company's earnings before interest and taxes (EBIT) by its fixed financial obligations. Lenders may use this ratio in assessing the risk of a loan and determining appropriate loan terms.

Fixed rate

A type of loan in which the interest rate remains the same for the entire term of the loan, providing stability for the borrower in knowing what their monthly payments will be. Fixed rate loans are often used for longer-term loans, such as mortgages or business loans.

Floating rate

A type of loan in which the interest rate is subject to change based on an index or benchmark, such as the prime rate or LIBOR. Floating rate loans can provide flexibility for borrowers, potentially resulting in lower interest costs over time.

Funding source

The means by which loan funds are obtained, which can include banks, credit unions, private investors, or the capital markets. The choice of funding source can impact the cost and terms of the loan, and should be carefully considered during the loan structuring process.

Funds flow statement

A financial statement that shows how a company's cash balance has changed over time, including all receipts and disbursements. Funds flow statements can help lenders better understand a borrower's cash flow and working capital needs.

Goodwill

Goodwill refers to the intangible value that a business or borrower has built up over time, such as a loyal customer base or a solid reputation. In loan structuring, goodwill may be used as collateral to secure a loan or as a factor in determining a borrower's creditworthiness. However, goodwill can be difficult to quantify and may not be seen as significant by lenders, making it less valuable than other forms of collateral.

Grace period

A grace period is a period of time after a loan payment is due during which the borrower is not penalized for making a late payment. The length of the grace period varies depending on the loan agreement and may be as short as a few days or as long as a few weeks. During the grace period, interest may still accumulate on the outstanding loan balance, which can result in larger payments due in the future.

Grace period interest

Grace period interest refers to the amount of interest that accrues on a loan during the grace period. While the borrower is not required to make a payment during the grace period, interest will continue to accumulate on the outstanding loan balance. Grace period interest may be added to the total principal balance of the loan and included in future payments.

Graduated payment loan

A graduated payment loan is a loan structure in which the borrower's payments start low and gradually increase over time. This type of loan may be used for installment loans, such as student loans, where the borrower's income is expected to increase over time. Graduated payment loans may also be used in commercial lending to help businesses during start-up and growth phases.

Graduated payment mortgage

A graduated payment mortgage is a loan structure in which the borrower's payments start low and gradually increase over time. This type of loan structure may appeal to borrowers who expect their income to increase in the future, allowing them to make larger payments later on. Graduated payment mortgages can be beneficial for borrowers who want to get into a home with a lower initial payment but can afford higher payments in the future.

Gross income

Gross income refers to the total income earned by an individual, business, or other entity before any deductions or taxes are taken out. In loan structuring, gross income may be used to determine a borrower's ability to repay a loan based on their income level. Gross income can include all sources of income, such as wages, investments, and rental income.

Group guarantee

A group guarantee is a loan structure in which multiple borrowers apply for a loan together and agree to guarantee the loan for each other. This type of loan structure may be used to help borrowers with poor credit or insufficient collateral secure loans from traditional lenders. Group guarantees may also come with more flexible repayment terms and lower interest rates than traditional loans.

Guarantee

A guarantee is a legal promise made by a third-party lender to repay a loan in the event that the borrower is unable to make scheduled payments. Guarantees are often required by lenders to reduce the risk of default and increase the odds of repayment by securing the loan. Guarantees can be secured, where the guarantor puts up a security or pledged asset, or unsecured, where the guarantor simply promises to repay the loan on the borrower's behalf.

Guaranteed loan

A guaranteed loan is a loan that is backed by a government agency or other third-party guarantee program. This type of loan structure may be used to help borrowers with poor credit or insufficient collateral secure loans from traditional lenders. Guaranteed loans may also come with more flexible repayment terms and lower interest rates than traditional loans.

Guarantor

A guarantor is a third-party individual or entity that promises to repay a loan on behalf of the borrower if the borrower is unable to make payments. Guarantors may be required by lenders to reduce the risk of default and increase the odds of repayment. Guarantors may also be used to help borrowers with poor credit scores secure loans by providing additional security to the lender.

Haircut

Haircut refers to the percentage reduction in the market value of a borrower's assets that a lender requires before it agrees to make a loan. For example, if a borrower needs a $50,000 loan and has $100,000 worth of assets, and the lender requires a 20% haircut, the borrower would receive a loan for $40,000 (20% of $100,000 is $20,000, which is subtracted from the $50,000 loan amount). Haircuts are common in loan structuring to protect lenders from the risk of the value of collateral assets falling below the value of the loan.

Hard money lending

Hard money lending is a type of loan that is backed by the value of a borrower's collateral, typically real estate. Hard money loans are often used to finance real estate investments and are typically short-term and high-interest. Loan structuring for hard money loans includes determining the value of the collateral and calculating the appropriate interest rate to compensate for the higher risk of default.

Hedge fund

Hedge fund is an investment fund that uses a variety of different strategies, such as leveraging and short-selling, to generate high returns for investors. Hedge funds often borrow money to increase their investments, and the loan structuring for these loans can involve complex instruments such as collateralized debt obligations.

High-yield debt

High-yield debt is a type of bond or loan that has a higher risk of default and a higher interest rate than investment-grade debt. High-yield debt is also known as junk bonds, and is typically issued by companies that have less-than-stellar creditworthiness. Loan structuring for high-yield debt involves higher interest rates to compensate for the greater risk of default.

Holdback

Holdback is a term used in loan structuring to refer to a portion of loan proceeds that are held back by the lender until certain conditions are met, such as the completion of a project or the successful sale of a property. Holdbacks are used to protect lenders from the risk of the borrower defaulting on the loan before the project or deal is complete.

Home equity loan

A home equity loan is a type of loan that uses a borrower's home as collateral. Loan structuring for home equity loans involves determining the value of the collateral (the borrower's home) and calculating a suitable interest rate based on the borrower's creditworthiness and the risk of default.

Hurdle rate

Hurdle rate is the minimum rate of return required by a lender or investor before investing in a loan or project. It is also known as the required rate of return. The hurdle rate is used to determine whether a loan or project is profitable enough to meet the lender's or investor's investment criteria. The hurdle rate is typically determined by a variety of factors including the risk of the investment, the lender's or investor's alternative investment opportunities, and the type of loan or project.

Hybrid securities

Hybrid securities are financial instruments that have characteristics of both debt and equity. Loan structuring for hybrid securities can involve convertible bonds, which can be converted into equity at a later date, or preferred shares, which have fixed dividend payments but can also appreciate in value.

Inflation

The rate at which the general level of prices for goods and services is rising, and, subsequently, the purchasing power of currency is falling. Inflation can affect loan structuring by reducing the real value of the loan amount over time, which should be taken into consideration when setting the loan term and repayment schedule.

Interest Rates

The amount of money charged by a lender to a borrower for the use of borrowed money. The interest rate is typically expressed as a percentage of the total loan amount and can be either fixed or variable. It is an important factor to consider when structuring a loan as it affects the total amount of money the borrower will need to repay.

Interest-Only Loan

A loan in which the borrower only pays the interest due for a certain period, typically between 5 and 10 years, before starting to repay the principal. This type of loan may be useful in certain situations, such as when the borrower expects to receive a large income in the future, but can also be risky if the borrower is not prepared to make principal payments when due.

J-Curve Effect

Refers to the initial period when cash outflows (loan repayment) exceed cash inflows (loan payments) for a new investment or business venture until the investment starts generating returns.

Joint Development Agreement (JDA)

A popular strategy for real estate developers to combine their resources, experience, and expertise to develop and manage projects.

Joint Lead Arranger (JLA)

In loan syndication, the joint lead arranger works alongside the lead arranger and helps secure other lending banks to invest in the loan.

Joint Ventures

A business arrangement where two or more parties come together to develop, finance and operate a mutually beneficial venture.

Judgment Lien

A court-ordered lien placed on a borrower's property as part of a judgment issued by a judge.

Jumbo Loan

A jumbo loan is a type of home loan that exceeds the typical dollar amount for conventional loan limits established by Fannie Mae and Freddie Mac.

Junior and Senior Debt

Junior debt is a higher risk loan that is paid after senior debt in cases of default. Senior debt, on the other hand, is the predominant loan that has priority over all other debts for repayment.

Junior Loan

It refers to a subordinate loan that has much lower priority in terms of repayments as compared to other senior loans. The junior loans are often accompanied by a higher interest rate as compared to the senior loan.

Junior Mezzanine Debt

This is one of the riskiest forms of debt financing that provides a quicker payback to the investors with a higher interest rate.

Just-in-Time (JIT) Inventory

A popular production methodology practiced by firms to minimize inventory costs by ordering and receiving goods when they are needed in the production process, eliminating the need for storage space, and reducing the risk of inventory-related losses.

Keeping covenants

Keeping covenants refers to the borrower's compliance with the terms and conditions of the loan agreement. In loan structuring, the lender includes covenants in the loan agreement to ensure that the borrower is taking the necessary steps to repay the loan. By keeping covenants, the borrower shows that they are a reliable partner and reduces the risk of default.

Keepwell Agreement

A Keepwell Agreement is an agreement wherein a parent company guarantees the performance of its subsidiary's debts. In loan structuring, a Keepwell Agreement establishes a connection between the borrower and the parent company to give confidence to the lender that the borrower will be able to repay the loan.

Key performance ratio (KPR)

A key performance ratio is a financial metric used to evaluate the performance of a company. The KPRs are used to identify the strengths and weaknesses of the company and help lenders determine the risk associated with the loan. In loan structuring, using KPRs helps lenders evaluate the company's capacity to repay the loan.

Key person events (KPE)

KPEs are events that can trigger a reduction in the amount of the loan or restructuring of the terms for existing loans. Such events can include the disability or death of a key borrower or guarantor or the termination or resignation of a key member of the management team. In loan structuring, the KPE provisions protect the interests of the lender by ensuring that the borrower is still capable of repaying the loan even with a change in key personnel.

Kicker

A kicker is an additional clause that is added to a loan agreement to provide the lender with an extra incentive for lending. Kickers provide the lender with equity participation, either in company ownership or revenue sharing, if the company performs well. In loan structuring, kickers act as a safeguard for the lender to recover their investment in case the borrower defaults.

Kicker provision

A kicker provision is an agreement to provide the lender with additional compensation or equity participation in exchange for better loan terms. In loan structuring, the kicker provision incentivizes the lender to provide better loan terms by giving them an additional benefit.

Kick-out rights

Kick-out rights allow the lender to remove certain investors from the loan agreement if they do not meet certain conditions. The lender can use these rights to enforce the terms of the loan and protect their interests. In loan structuring, the kick-out rights act as a safeguard for the lender to ensure that the investors are committed to the loan.

Kiting

Kiting is a fraudulent activity where a borrower inflates the balance of one account and then transfers the excess funds to a second account. This gives the impression that the second account has more capital than it actually does. In loan structuring, kiting is a red flag for lenders as it signals a risk of default.

Know Your Customer (KYC)

Know Your Customer is a process where the lender verifies the identity of the borrower to comply with anti-money laundering laws. KYC is essential in loan structuring, as it helps lenders avoid fraudulent activities and reduce the risk of default. The process includes verifying the borrower's identity, verifying their sources of funds, and understanding their financial situation.

KPI-based lending

Key performance indicators (KPIs) are used to evaluate the performance of a company. In KPI-based lending, the loan agreement specifies certain KPIs that the borrower must meet to remain eligible for the loan or receive better terms. This helps lenders monitor the performance of the borrower and reduce the risk of default.

Leverage

Leverage is the amount of debt that a borrower has relative to their assets, and it plays a key role in loan structuring. High levels of leverage can be risky, particularly if the borrower does not have sufficient cash flow or liquidity to service the debt.

Liquidity

Liquidity is the ability of a borrower to access cash quickly and easily, either through a credit line or by selling assets. Good liquidity is important in loan structuring because it provides a safety net in case of unexpected events.

Loan Amortization

Loan Amortization is the process of paying off a loan in equal installments over a specified period of time. It involves calculating the amount of each payment based on the size of the loan, the interest rate, and the repayment period.

Loan Covenants

Loan Covenants are legal agreements between a borrower and a lender that outline specific terms and conditions that the borrower must meet in order to keep the loan in good standing. Common loan covenants include requirements for maintaining certain financial ratios, for providing regular financial statements, and for limiting the amount of additional debt that the borrower may take on.

Loan Document

Loan Document is the legal agreement between a borrower and a lender that outlines the terms and conditions of the loan, including the amount, interest rate, repayment period, and any other requirements.

Loan Modification

Loan Modification is the process of changing the terms of an existing loan, either to make it more affordable for the borrower or to mitigate the risk for the lender. It may involve extending the repayment period, reducing the interest rate, or adjusting the amount of the loan.

Loan Origination

Loan Origination is the process of creating a new loan, from the initial application to the disbursement of funds. It involves assessing the borrower's creditworthiness, evaluating the collateral, and negotiating the terms of the loan.

Loan Servicing

Loan Servicing is the process of managing a loan after it has been disbursed, including collecting payments, providing customer service to the borrower, and working with the borrower to resolve any issues that may arise. Good loan servicing is important in loan structuring because it can help ensure that the borrower remains in good standing and that the lender receives timely payments.

Loan Structuring

Loan Structuring is the process of designing a loan that meets the needs of both the borrower and the lender. It involves determining the amount of the loan, the interest rate, the repayment period, and any other terms and conditions that will be imposed on the loan, such as collateral requirements, fees, and covenants.

Loan Syndication

Loan Syndication is the process of pooling funds from multiple lenders to finance a large loan. It involves structuring the loan so that each lender has a specific role and a specific level of risk.

Margin

The amount added to the index rate that determines the interest rate on a loan. The margin is determined based on factors like the borrower's creditworthiness, loan amount, and repayment period, and can vary among lenders.

Maturity Date

The date on which a loan agreement is set to be fully repaid, including principal and interest accrued. The maturity date is usually specified in the loan agreement and each periodic payment made towards the loan reduces the outstanding balance until the loan is fully repaid on the agreed-upon date.

Mezzanine Financing

A type of financing used to fill the gap between senior secured debt and equity investment in a company's capital structure. Mezzanine financing typically involves higher interest rates and equity participation than senior debt, and does not require collateral like traditional debt financing.

Modified Internal Rate of Return (MIRR)

A financial metric used to determine the rate of return on a loan with irregular cash flows. MIRR accounts for the timing and size of cash flows and assumes that interim payments are reinvested at a specified rate.

Mortgage

A loan that is secured by real estate, such as a house or commercial property. The borrower provides the property as collateral and the lender has the right to foreclose on the property if the borrower defaults on the loan.

Mortgage Broker

An individual or company that acts as an intermediary between borrowers and lenders in the mortgage lending process. Mortgage brokers help borrowers find suitable lenders and loan products and may negotiate terms on behalf of the borrower.

Mortgage Servicing

The process of collecting loan payments, managing escrow accounts, and handling other administrative tasks related to mortgage loans. Mortgage servicers are often different from the original lender and may be hired by the lender to handle loan servicing tasks.

Multiple Advance Loan

A loan that provides for multiple disbursements of funds over time. Multiple advance loans are typically used for construction or renovation projects, and disbursements are made as-needed based on the completion of specified project milestones.

Municipal Bond

A type of bond issued by state and local governments to finance public projects or infrastructure. Municipal bonds are exempt from federal income tax and may also be exempt from state or local income tax in some cases.

Must-vs.Want Analysis

A financial analysis tool used to measure the feasibility of a loan or investment project. Must-vs.-want analysis compares the minimum requirements or "musts" of a project to the discretionary or optional aspects, known as "wants", to determine if the project is financially viable. The analysis may include factors such as project costs, projected revenue, and market demand.

NDA

Non-Disclosure Agreement (NDA) is a legal contract that prevents one or both parties from disclosing confidential information to third parties. In the context of loans, an NDA may be used to protect borrower information or lender trade secrets.

Negative covenant

A clause in a loan agreement that restricts the borrower's actions or imposes obligations on the borrower. Examples can include restrictions on the borrower's ability to incur additional debt or distribute profits to shareholders.

Negotiable

A negotiable loan is a loan for which the terms can be changed through negotiation between the borrower and lender. This can include changes to the interest rate, size of the loan, or repayment terms. Negotiable loans may be more flexible than non-negotiable loans, but they also carry more risk for the lender.

Net Present Value

A financial calculation used by lenders and borrowers to determine the current value of future loan payments. It takes into consideration factors such as the time value of money, the interest rate, and the length of the loan. The higher the net present value, the more attractive the loan is for a borrower.

NOI

Net Operating Income (NOI) is a calculation used in commercial real estate to measure the profitability of rental properties. NOI is calculated by subtracting operating expenses from total rental income. It does not include debt payments or taxes. Lenders may use NOI when evaluating the risk of a loan for a commercial property purchase.

Non-amortizing loan

A loan where the borrower only pays back the interest on the principal. The principal remains the same throughout the loan term, and the borrower is responsible for repaying the principal in full at the end of the loan term. This type of loan is often used for short-term financing needs.

Non-performing loan

A loan that is in default, or has been in arrears for a specified length of time. These loans are typically considered to have a higher risk of not being repaid in full. Lenders may try to sell non-performing loans to collection agencies or other investors.

Non-recourse loan

A type of loan where the lender's only source of repayment is the collateral securing the loan. In the case of default, the lender cannot go after the borrower's personal assets or income. This type of loan is often used for commercial real estate purchases, where the property itself serves as collateral.

Note

A debt instrument that evidences a specific amount owed by the borrower to the lender. It includes details such as the repayment terms, interest rate, and collateral. The borrower signs the note as a promise to repay the loan according to the specified terms.

Notice of default

A formal notice sent by a lender to a borrower when the borrower has failed to make a payment on time or has otherwise violated the loan agreement. The notice outlines the consequences of the default, such as penalties or foreclosure. The borrower typically has a set period of time to cure the default before the lender takes further action.

Obligor

The entity or individual who is responsible for repaying a loan. This term is commonly used in bond and loan agreements. The obligor is required to make the repayments on the loan on time and in full, including any interest and fees that may apply.

Offshore

A term used to describe loans made to borrowers in foreign countries. These loans are often made by multinational financial institutions and are subject to international laws and regulations.

Open-End Mortgage

A type of mortgage that allows the borrower to borrow additional funds under specific conditions. An open-end mortgage is similar to a home equity line of credit (HELOC) and is often used for construction financing.

Operating Covenants

A set of conditions that a borrower must follow to ensure that the operations of the business are conducted in a reasonable manner. These covenants typically place restrictions on the borrower's ability to take certain actions, such as selling assets or entering into new contracts, without first seeking approval from the lender.

Operating Expense Escalation

A provision in a lease agreement that allows the landlord to pass on increases in operating expenses to the tenant. This provision typically requires the tenant to pay a pro-rata share of any increase in expenses associated with running the property, such as property taxes, insurance, and maintenance costs.

Option

A contractual right, but not the obligation, to take a specific action at some point in the future. In loan structuring, options are commonly used to provide borrowers with flexibility in their repayment schedules.

Origination Fee

A fee charged by lenders to cover the costs of processing a loan application. Typically a percentage of the loan amount, this fee is charged upfront and is non-refundable even if the loan application is denied. The origination fee covers the lender's administrative expenses, credit check, and underwriting costs.

Overage

The amount by which the loan commitment exceeds the actual amount borrowed by the borrower. For instance, if a lender commits to providing a loan of $10 million but the borrower only uses $8 million, the overage is $2 million. This term is commonly used in commercial real estate lending.

Over-Collateralization

A technique used in loan structuring where the value of collateral pledged by the borrower is greater than the loan amount. This provides lenders with additional security in case the borrower defaults on the loan. Over-collateralization is commonly used in asset-backed securities to enhance credit quality.

Overriding Royalty Interest

A type of royalty paid to a third party based on the production of minerals or other natural resources. This type of royalty is often used in loan agreements secured by mineral rights. The overriding royalty interest holder is entitled to receive a percentage of the profits from the sale of the resources produced.

Participation Loan

A loan in which multiple lenders provide funding for a single borrower. Each lender has a proportional share in the loan and is entitled to a portion of the interest and principal payments.

Payment Default

A situation in which the borrower fails to make a scheduled loan payment. Payment defaults can result in late fees, increased interest rates, and damage to the borrower's credit score.

Payment Schedule

The predetermined schedule of payments that a borrower must make to repay the loan in full. The schedule typically includes the amount, frequency, and due date of each payment.

Personal Guarantee

A promise by an individual to repay a loan if the borrower is unable to do so. Personal guarantees are often required for small business loans and other types of high-risk lending.

Prepayment Penalty

A fee charged by a lender if the borrower pays off the loan before the end of the term. The penalty is intended to compensate the lender for the loss of interest they would have earned if the loan had continued.

Prequalification

The process by which a lender evaluates a borrower's creditworthiness and ability to repay a loan. Prequalification is typically done before a borrower submits a loan application.

Pricing

The interest rate charged on a loan, as well as any fees or charges associated with the loan. The pricing of a loan is based on factors such as the borrower's creditworthiness and the perceived risk of the loan.

Principal

The amount of money borrowed from a lender that must be repaid. The principal amount is used to calculate the interest charged on the loan.

Project Financing

A loan specifically designed to finance a particular project, such as the construction of a building or the development of a new product. The structure of a project financing loan is usually based on the cash flow generated by the project itself.

Put Option

A provision in a loan agreement that allows the borrower to sell the loan back to the lender at a predetermined price. Put options can be used to protect against changes in interest rates or other market conditions.

Qualified Institutional Buyer (QIB)

This is a type of investor that is exempt from certain SEC registration requirements. QIBs are typically large institutions (such as banks, insurance companies, and pension funds) that have a minimum of $100 million in assets.

Qualified Mortgage

A qualified mortgage is a type of loan that meets certain criteria established by the Consumer Financial Protection Bureau. A qualified mortgage offers greater legal protections for lenders and borrowers, and generally requires a borrower to have a DTI ratio of 43% or less.

Qualifying Ratios

These are calculations used by lenders to determine a borrower's ability to repay a loan. The two ratios typically used are the debt-to-income ratio (DTI) and loan-to-value ratio (LTV). The DTI ratio measures the percentage of a borrower's monthly income that goes towards debt repayment, while the LTV ratio measures the percentage of the loan amount against the value of the collateral.

Quality of Collateral

This refers to the value and marketability of the assets that are used to secure a loan. Lenders will typically conduct a collateral assessment to determine the quality of collateral, which will impact the loan terms and interest rate offered.

Quarterly Payment

This is a form of loan repayment in which the borrower makes payments every three months. Quarterly payments are popular in some industries, such as agricultural or seasonal businesses, where cash flow is less predictable.

Quasi-Equity

This is a type of financing that shares some characteristics with equity and some with debt. Quasi-equity is typically used in leveraged buyouts, and can be structured as preferred equity, convertible debt, or mezzanine debt. Quasi-equity offers the borrower some flexibility in repayment terms and may provide more favorable tax treatment than pure debt financing.

Quick Ratio

This is a calculation used by lenders to assess a company's ability to meet short-term debt obligations. The quick ratio measures a company's liquid assets (such as cash, marketable securities, and accounts receivable) against its short-term liabilities (such as accounts payable and accrued expenses).

Quiet Period

In the context of loan structuring, the quiet period is a period of time during which the borrower is prohibited from discussing details of the loan with potential investors. This is typically a requirement for publicly listed companies that are seeking financing.

Quota Share

This is a type of loan syndication in which each lender is responsible for a specific percentage of the loan. For example, if a $100 million loan is syndicated with a 50% quota share, each lender would be responsible for $50 million of the loan.

Quoted Margin

This is the additional interest rate added to a loan's variable interest rate. Quoted margin is usually added as a percentage or point value, and is determined by the lender based on an assessment of the borrower's creditworthiness and the overall risk of the loan.

Rate Lock

A rate lock is an agreement between a borrower and lender that fixes the interest rate on a loan for a set period of time. This is typically done to prevent interest rates from rising during the application process, giving the borrower time to complete the loan without worrying about market fluctuations.

Refinancing

Refinancing is the process of replacing an existing loan with a new one. It is often done to take advantage of lower interest rates or to change the terms of the loan. Refinancing can save borrowers money in the long run, but it can also result in higher costs if the new loan has a longer term or higher interest rate than the original loan.

Regulatory Compliance

Regulatory compliance refers to the process of ensuring that a loan meets all applicable laws, rules, and regulations. This includes everything from state and federal lending laws to consumer protection laws and data privacy regulations. Failing to comply with these regulations can result in fines, legal action, and reputational damage for lenders.

Repayment Schedule

A repayment schedule is a document that outlines how a borrower will repay a loan. It includes the amount of each payment, the date it is due, and the interest rate being charged. The repayment schedule is usually provided to the borrower at the time the loan is made and serves as a guide for making payments over time.

Residual Value

Residual value refers to the estimated value of a piece of collateral (such as a vehicle) at the end of the loan term. Lenders use residual value to determine the amount of the loan and the monthly payments. If the borrower defaults on the loan, the lender may repossess the collateral and sell it in order to recover any outstanding debt.

Restructuring

Loan restructuring is a process that involves making changes to the terms of a loan in order to make it more manageable for the borrower. This may include extending the loan term, changing the interest rate or payment schedule, or reducing the amount of the loan. Loan restructuring can help borrowers avoid default and maintain a good credit rating.

Revolving Credit

Revolving credit is a type of loan that allows borrowers to access a set amount of funds on an as-needed basis. Unlike traditional loans that are paid back in installments, revolving credit can be used and repaid over and over again as long as the borrower stays within the credit limit.

Right of Rescission

The right of rescission is a provision under federal law that gives borrowers the right to cancel certain types of loans within a certain period of time (usually three days). This applies to loans taken out for personal or household use, but does not apply to loans used to purchase real estate or business loans.

Risk Assessment

Risk assessment is the process of evaluating the potential risks associated with a loan. This includes assessing the likelihood of default, the borrower's credit history, and the overall economic conditions that may impact the borrower's ability to repay the loan.

Risk-Based Pricing

Risk-based pricing is a strategy used by lenders to charge borrowers different interest rates based on their perceived level of risk. Borrowers with higher credit scores and better credit histories may qualify for lower interest rates, while those with lower credit scores or a history of defaults may be charged higher rates.

Securitization

The process of turning financial assets into securities that can be sold to investors, with the aim of transferring the risk associated with those assets away from the originator.

Seniority

The order in which different debts are paid off in the event of a borrower defaulting on their loan. Senior debt has priority over junior debt.

Servicer

A third-party organization responsible for administering the collection of payments, management of assets, and maintenance of records for a loan facility.

Special purpose vehicle (SPV)

A legal entity that is created specifically to hold and manage a set of assets for a specific purpose, often used in securitization transactions.

Standby letter of credit

A type of financial guarantee provided by a bank or other financial institution, typically used to ensure that a borrower will fulfill their payment obligations.

Structured finance

A financial instrument that is created by pooling various financial assets, such as loans or mortgages, to form a security that can be bought and sold.

Subordination

The act of prioritizing one debt over another, typically for the purpose of reducing risk for certain lenders or investors.

Swap

An agreement between two parties to exchange payment streams based on predetermined terms, usually used to hedge against interest rate or currency risk.

Syndication

The process of involving multiple lenders in a loan facility, where each lender provides a portion of the overall loan amount, thereby reducing the risk for any one lender.

Synthetic securitization

A type of securitization that involves the creation of artificial securities to replicate the cash flows of a pool of assets, without actually transferring ownership of those assets.

Takeout Financing

Takeout financing is a type of loan used to replace an existing loan, typically a short-term loan, with longer-term financing. Takeout financing is often used in real estate development projects, where a short-term construction loan is replaced by longer-term financing once the project is completed. The term "takeout" refers to the fact that the new loan "takes out" the old loan.

Tax Equity Financing

Tax equity financing is a type of financing used in renewable energy projects, such as wind and solar farms. Tax equity financing involves a tax equity investor providing financing to a project in exchange for tax credits associated with the project. The tax credits are then used to offset the tax liability of the tax equity investor.

Term Loan

A term loan is a type of loan that is structured with a fixed interest rate and a set repayment period, usually between one and ten years. Term loans are commonly used for financing large projects, such as real estate development or business expansion. The interest rate on a term loan is typically lower than that of a short-term loan, and the repayment period is longer, making it easier for the borrower to manage their debt load.

Term Sheet

A term sheet is a document used in loan structuring that outlines the key terms of a loan, including interest rate, repayment period, collateral, and any other conditions of the loan. The term sheet is typically non-binding, meaning that it is not a definitive agreement, but rather a starting point for negotiations between the lender and borrower.

Term to Maturity

Term to maturity is a term used in loan structuring to describe the length of time until a loan reaches its maturity date, at which point the borrower must repay the full principal amount of the loan. The term to maturity is typically measured in years and is an important factor in determining the overall risk of the loan.

Total Debt Service Ratio

The Total Debt Service Ratio (TDSR) is a ratio used by lenders to determine if a borrower has the ability to repay their loan. The TDSR takes into account the borrower's income, debt obligations, and other financial commitments, and calculates the percentage of their income required to service their debt. A TDSR of 40% or lower is generally considered acceptable by lenders, as it indicates that the borrower has enough income to comfortably manage their debt payments.

Trade Finance

Trade finance is a type of financing used to facilitate international trade transactions. Trade finance typically involves loans, lines of credit, or other financing instruments that help importers and exporters manage the risk associated with international trade, such as currency fluctuations, political instability, and shipping delays.

Tranche

A Tranche is a term used in loan structuring that refers to a portion of a loan that is separated into multiple layers of risk. Each layer has a different interest rate, repayment term, and collateral. The purpose of the tranche is to attract investors with differing risk tolerance levels, increasing the potential pool of investors for the loan. The different layers of risk associated with each tranche create a more complex loan structure, but it spreads the risk among the different investors, minimizing the overall risk of the loan.

Transitional Financing

Transitional financing is a type of loan that is used to bridge the gap between a company's current financial situation and its desired state in the future. For example, a company may use transitional financing to fund a major expansion or acquisition, with the goal of increasing its revenue and profitability. Transitional financing can be structured as a term loan or a line of credit, and typically has a higher interest rate than traditional financing.

Trust Receipt

A trust receipt is a document used in trade finance that allows a buyer to take possession of goods before they are paid for. The trust receipt acts as a security instrument, giving the lender a security interest in the goods until the buyer pays for them. Trust receipts are commonly used in cross-border transactions, where there may be a delay between the shipment of goods and their arrival at the destination.

Undefined Default (UD)

A failure to make a payment on a loan, or otherwise comply with the terms of the loan agreement, that is not specifically covered by the loan documents. This may include events such as the borrower's insolvency, or the occurrence of a natural disaster that affects the underlying collateral.

Underleveraged

A company that has the capacity to take on more debt but chooses not to, or has a lower debt-to-equity ratio than its peers. This makes the company less risky to lenders and potentially more attractive to investors.

Underlying Asset

The asset that is secured by a loan or other financial agreement, such as real estate or equipment. The value of the underlying asset is used to determine the amount of the loan, and provides a source of collateral to the lender in case of default.

Underwriting

The process by which the lender assesses the risk of granting a loan, including the borrower's creditworthiness and the ability to repay. This involves evaluating financial statements, credit reports, and other relevant documents to determine the borrower's ability to meet the loan obligations, and ultimately decide if the loan should be approved or not.

Uniform Commercial Code (UCC)

A set of legal guidelines for commercial transactions, including lending and borrowing, that have been adopted in all 50 states. The UCC provides a consistent framework and language for financial contracts, including security agreements and loan documents.

Unitranche

A type of loan structure that combines senior and subordinated debt into a single facility, with a single interest rate and repayment schedule. This structure is often used in middle-market financing and allows for easier loan administration and management.

Unsecured Loan

A loan that is not backed by collateral or assets, and is therefore riskier for the lender. Unsecured loans typically have higher interest rates compared to secured loans, as the lender assumes a greater risk.

Upfront Fees

Fees paid to the lender at the outset of the loan, in addition to interest payments. These may include origination fees, commitment fees, and other transaction fees, and are usually calculated as a percentage of the total loan amount.

Upstream Security

A type of security agreement in which the borrower pledges assets that are owned by a subsidiary, but are upstream from the borrower. This means that the collateral is owned by an entity that is higher up in the corporate structure, and therefore may be subject to competing claims or other restrictions.

Used to Fund (UTF)

A term used to describe a collateral package that is backing a commercial loan. The UTF represents the types and values of the assets used to secure the loan, and typically includes detailed information about the asset's condition, location, and other relevant details.

Vacant Land Loan

A vacant land loan is a form of loan structuring where the borrower borrows money to purchase undeveloped land. Vacant land loans can have different terms, interest rates, and repayment schedules, depending on the lender's requirements and the borrower's creditworthiness. It is essential to have a well-structured agreement that outlines the terms and conditions of the loan.

Valuation

It is the process of determining the value of an asset or property. It plays a critical role in loan structuring and impacts the loan amount and interest rate. Valuation is usually conducted by an independent party and takes into account factors such as market trends, condition, location, and comparables.

Variable Interest Rate

A variable interest rate is a loan interest rate that fluctuates based on market conditions, such as the prime rate or LIBOR (London Interbank Offered Rate). Variable interest rates can be beneficial to borrowers as they can take advantage of lower interest rates, but it can also increase the risk of rising interest rates and higher monthly payments.

Variable Term

A variable term refers to the length of time the borrower has to repay the loan, which can vary depending on market conditions and other factors. A variable term can be beneficial to borrowers who need flexibility in their payment schedule or anticipate changes in their financial situation. However, a variable term can also increase the risk of higher interest rates and longer repayment periods.

Vendor Financing

It is a form of loan structuring where the vendor (seller) provides financing to the buyer, instead of traditional lenders such as banks. Vendor financing can be beneficial to both parties, where the buyer can get financing at a lower interest rate and the vendor can sell the property faster, achieving a competitive advantage. It is essential to have a well-structured agreement that outlines the terms, interest rate, repayment schedule, and default consequences.

Vendor Takeback Mortgage

A vendor takeback mortgage is a form of loan structuring where the seller of a property provides financing to the buyer. It is usually a second mortgage and can be beneficial to both parties. The buyer can get additional financing at a lower interest rate, and the seller can sell the property faster, at a higher price. Vendor takeback mortgages can have different terms such as interest rate, repayment schedule, and default consequences.

Venture Capitalist

A venture capitalist is a person or a firm that invests in small companies or startups in exchange for a share of ownership. Venture capitalists can be beneficial to startups by providing necessary funding, expertise, and a network of contacts. In loan structuring, venture capitalists can be an alternative source of financing when traditional lenders are not available.

Verification of Deposit (VOD)

Verification of deposit is a process of verifying the borrower's bank deposits and balance. Lenders require VOD to ensure that the borrower has sufficient funds to repay the loan and to verify the source of down payment. VOD can be done through various methods such as contacting the borrower's bank or using a third-party service.

Verification of Employment (VOE)

Verification of employment is a process of verifying the borrower's employment status and income. Lenders require VOE to ensure that the borrower has a stable income source and can repay the loan. VOE can be done through various methods such as contacting the borrower's employer or using a third-party service.

Veterans Affairs (VA) Loan

A VA loan is a form of loan structuring that is available to eligible veterans, active-duty personnel, and surviving spouses. The VA loan program is designed to assist veterans in purchasing a home with favorable terms such as no down payment and no private mortgage insurance. VA loans can have different terms, interest rates, and repayment schedules, depending on the lender's requirements and the borrower's creditworthiness.

Waiver

Waiver refers to the relinquishment of the borrower's legal rights or any other contractual rights. It is an essential aspect of loan structuring, especially when dealing with collaterals. A waiver can be granted to the borrower to enable them to use the collateral in other transactions. It is vital to consider the implications of waivers while loan structuring to ensure proper management of collaterals.

Weighted Average Coupon

Weighted Average Coupon refers to the average interest rate paid on a pool of loans. WAC is calculated by taking the coupon on each loan and multiplying it by the proportion of the pool that each loan represents. It is vital to consider WAC while loan structuring as it helps in identifying the level of risk associated with the loan portfolio.

Whole Loan Purchase

Whole Loan Purchase refers to the process of buying an entire loan instead of investing in a portion of it. It is a common practice in loan structuring, especially in the case of mortgage loans. A whole loan purchase is usually done by investors who want to take a more significant stake in the loan portfolio. It is essential to understand whole loan purchase to ensure that the loan portfolio is balanced.

Wholesale Lending

Wholesale Lending refers to the practice of lending money to other financial institutions such as banks or credit unions instead of individual borrowers. This type of lending is usually done at a lower interest rate, and the loan amount can be substantial. It is vital to understand Wholesale Lending for successful loan structuring as it offers an opportunity for institutional investors to earn fixed income by lending money to other institutions.

Working Capital

Working Capital refers to the financial resources that are available to a business for day-to-day operations. It is the difference between the company's current assets and its current liabilities. This means that working capital is the amount of money a business has available to pay for wages, rent, and other expenses. It is essential to have enough working capital to avoid any financial difficulty that might arise. Proper loan structuring can help a business to maintain a healthy level of working capital.

Working Group

Working Group refers to a team of experts who are responsible for loan structuring activities in a financial institution. They have expertise in various aspects of lending such as credit analysis, legal documentation, and compliance. The working group ensures that the loan is structured in a way that mitigates any risks associated with the borrowing. They are also responsible for documenting and monitoring the loan.

Working Interest

Working Interest refers to the ownership interest, usually in an oil or gas property or similar asset. The working interest owner is usually responsible for a share of the expenses associated with the asset or property. It is vital to consider working interest while loan structuring to determine the borrower's ability to repay the loan, especially in the energy sector.

Workout

Workout refers to the process of negotiating and restructuring a loan for a borrower who is unable to make payments or is in default. Workout is an essential aspect of loan structuring as it can help in salvaging a loan that would have otherwise been lost. The workout process typically involves negotiations between the lender and the borrower, and it may result in a change of terms, credit agreement, or payment plans.

Write-down

Write-down refers to the decrease in the value of an asset as a result of a decline in its market value or due to any other factors such as aging. It is essential to consider write-down while loan structuring to ensure that the lender has enough collateral to cover the loan amount in case of the borrower's default. A write-down can impact the credit rating of a borrower adversely, hence the importance of careful loan structuring.

Write-Off

Write-Off refers to the cancellation of a debt due to the borrower's default or any other reasons such as bankruptcy. It is critical to consider the possibility of a write-off while loan structuring to mitigate risks associated with the borrower's default. Write-offs can adversely impact the lender's finances hence the significance of careful loan structuring.

Yield

Yield is the income that an investor receives from an investment, usually expressed as a percentage of the investment's cost. For bonds, this is often the annual interest rate that the bond's issuer has agreed to pay. Yield reflects not only the coupon payments, but also the difference between the purchase price and the bond's eventual redemption value.

Yield Curve

A Yield Curve is a graph that shows the relationship between bond yields and maturities. It generally shows the yields for bonds of similar credit quality, such as US Treasuries, plotting the yields along the x-axis with the term of the bond on the y-axis. The curve may take on different shapes, including an upward or downward sloping curve, or a flat curve. The shape of the Yield Curve can offer insight into the expectations for future economic growth and inflation.

Yield Curve Steepening

Yield Curve Steepening occurs when the spread between short-term and long-term interest rates increases, making the Yield Curve steeper. This can occur when economic conditions suggest that inflation or economic growth may pick up in the future, thereby leading to higher long-term rates. Yield Curve Steepening can affect many aspects of the bond market and can influence the pricing of investments.

Yield Maintenance

Yield Maintenance is a type of prepayment penalty that borrowers may be charged if they wish to pay off a loan early. This calculation is designed to make the lender whole for the loss of interest payments that would have been made had the loan been repaid on its original schedule.

Yield Spread

Yield Spread is the difference between the yields of two different types of bonds, generally those with different credit ratings or maturities. The Yield Spread can offer insight into the relative attractiveness of investing in one bond over another. For example, a large Yield Spread between two bonds of the same duration but different credit rating would indicate that the market views one of the bonds as higher risk.

Yield Variance

Yield Variance measures how the price of a bond might change as a result of a change in interest rates. This calculation involves estimating the bond's duration and convexity

Yield-on-Basis

Yield-on-Basis is the return on a bond, expressed in the form of a percentage of its price. This calculation takes into account the interest rate, the bond's coupon, and the bond's maturity. The result indicates the expected return on an investment in the bond over its lifetime.

Yield-to-Call

Yield-to-Call (YTC) is the expected return on a bond that will be called prior to maturity, considering the current market price, the call price, and the time remaining until the bond can be called. This calculation is done similarly to YTM, but takes into account that the bond may be called early, reducing the amount of time that the bondholder receives coupon payments.

Yield-to-Maturity

Yield-to-Maturity (YTM) is the calculation of the interest that a bond can bring you if it is held until it matures, taking into account the current market price, the coupon rate, and the time remaining until maturity. This calculation can get complicated for bonds that have more unusual coupon structures, like floating rates or multiple rate resets.

Yield-to-Worst

Yield-to-Worst (YTW) is the lowest potential yield that a bond can return, taking into account all of the possible outcomes